BareBackPress

This is a work of fiction. The characters, incidents, and dialogue are the products of the author's imagination and are not to be construed as real. Any resemblance to actual events or person, living or dead, is entirely coincidental.

BareBackPress
Hamilton, Ontario, Canada
For enquiries visit www.barebackpress.com
For information contact press@barebacklit.com
Cover layout and design by Choi Yunnam

No part of this can be used or reproduced in any manner whatsoever without written permission, except in the case of brief quotations embodied in critical articles and reviews. For information address BareBackPress.

COPYRIGHT © 2016 Wayne F. Burke
All RIGHTS RESERVED
ISBN-13: 978-1926449081
ISBN-10: 1926449088

INNARDS

One - 9
Turkey - 10
Last Supper - 12
Shot – 13
Naked – 14
Chicken – 16
Cousin – 17
Chipper – 18
Christmas Morn – 19
Two - 20
Moving Man – 21
The Stripper – 22
The Maid – 24
Three – 25
Wife-Beater – 26
Paddy Wagon – 27
Flustrated – 29
Maybe – 31
The Fix – 32
Four – 33
Moider – 34
Mush – 35
Savior – 36
Poison Gas – 37
Left Jab – 38
Any More Questions? – 39
9 Billion Years – 40
Nehru jackets – 41
Bait – 42
Five – 44
The Girl and the Greek – 45
Ma Cherie Amore – 46
Date – 47
Odd – 48
Boston Cream – 49
Six – 50

Water – 51
Spring Training – 52
Rights – 53
Okra – 54
Frozen – 55
Zero – 57
Rat Race – 58
The Sub-Mariner – 59
Snoop – 61
Pop – 62
NORTH – 63
Seven – 64
The Pier – 65
The Diner – 66
208$ – 67
Burke's Inn – 68
12:41 A.M. - 69
Advice – 70
Reality – 71
Voice – 72
Stopped – 73
Fragile – 74
Twilight – 75
2 Oh One – 76
Jackass – 77
Eight – 78
1:30 P.M. – 79
Same Oh – 80
Cheap Living – 81
Punk Fight – 82
Townie – 83
Backyard – 84
Slog – 85
Nine – 86
Wing Tips – 87
Descent to New York – 88
Notebook – 89
Art – 90

Hi-Ho – 91
Meck-A-Nick – 92
Exist – 93
Ten – 94
Lumbago – 95
Construction – 96
Creatures Come Out At Night – 97
Big Spender - 100

Dedicated to Uncle Earl
for his unconditional and unwavering support

KNUCKLE
Wayne F. Burke
SANDWICHES

1

Palm Sunday —
my brother and I
whip each other with palms

Turkey

The kids shouted as they
circled me on the
schoolyard play ground:
"turkey-gobble-gobble!
"turkey-gobble-gobble!"
It was Thanksgiving:
because I was a "Burke"
I was also a "Berkie"
which some evil kid had
translated to "Turkey,"
a name I disliked —
I was sensitive to
slights;
I ran at them and
they scattered
but shouted even louder,
a hellish chorus
faces gleeful with malice:
"turkey-gobble-gobble!"
One kid was slow to move
and I caught him with a punch;
he was in the retarded class
taught in the basement
and it was rumored he had a tapeworm.
We fought it out:
he was tough
and with a head hard as wood;
the fight went on a long time
before he said "I give."
Afterward, no one called me

"turkey" again,
not to my face
anyway.

Last Supper

In grammar school we were
alphabetized
and I sat behind the same kid
every year
the back of his head
his perfectly combed hair;
he invited me to his home
an apartment on the 2nd floor
neatly arranged as his hair
and his father
who worked in a shoe factory
agreed I could stay
for supper
and I was served a hot dog
that crunched when I bit into it
and tasted good,
unlike the pliable 5-inch specimen
of unnamed meat products
I got at home,
and the pretty mother
who had a crippled leg
asked
would I like another
and I said "yes"
and ate the last dog
which
they could not afford to give,
but I did not know that—
did not know why I was never invited back
either.

Shot

I need to take a pill
because
of allergies;
I used to get shots
when a kid and
went with Gramp
to the doc's
dog-faced Doctor Dworkin
his pretty and slender
nurse
I was friendly with
until the night she
stuck the needle in
without warning me
and I flinched
and the needle stuck,
she could not pull it out,
ouch
I had no use for her
after,
did not want the lollipop
that was offered me
either,
but Gramp insisted that
I take it.

Naked

The lion roared into
the hearts of everyone
in the theater
and the movie began,
Elvis, or The Three Stooges,
or, once, The Naked Prey
which scared me
Friday night
I had gone to meet
my new Junior High School friend
who did not show
and I sat by myself
in the dark
as half-naked dancing girls
shimmied on the screen
in coming attractions
that did not attract
but terrified me
I felt an aura of evil,
of adult-somethingness
beyond my seventh grade
understanding,
and then the movie
which featured the torture
and mutilation
of white men
who intruded into
darkest Africa,
and I stood up and
went out to the concession
run by the theater-owner's kindly-seeming
mother
only she was not as kindly-seeming

as on Saturday afternoons
she seemed Gypsy-like and strange
dressed all in black
and part
of the evil
I had stumbled into
and was in danger
of somehow
becoming a part of.

Chicken

The kid in the road
gets a funny look
on his face
when I do not slow
and he scoots aside
as I drive by
and I remember
Dicky
in the high school parking lot
early in the morning
how he hit the windshield
of my car
and went over the roof
and how I watched him
in the rear view mirror
drop
as if out of the sky
and how I stopped
and ran to him
asked if he was alright
and how he got up
and gave me a look
and began to limp
toward the school
and without even one
of his smart-assed remarks
and how
during homeroom period
I felt
when I heard my name
announced
over the intercom
by the vice-principle.

Cousin

He was at the skating rink
one night,
somebody's tall and lanky cousin
from another part of town,
and I did not like the look on
his face
and started a fight with him
while on skates
and charged in
and ate knuckle sandwiches
off his fists
and backed-off
and tried again
and got hammered
and could not get inside no
matter what I tired
and grew frustrated
and started to call him names
but nothing I said
got me any closer to
him
and I quit,
beaten
and feeling chastened
because the kid had arms like
toothpicks
and was so thin
he looked like he would blow away
in a big wind.

Chipper

I pulled back the rubber band
of the slingshot
and hit the chipmunk
with a rock
and the chipmunk flopped
about on top of
a stone wall
and
to put it out of its misery
I beat it with a stick
but the thing would not
die
and I beat it some more
but
still alive
and I began to cry
and
beat it again
and again
saying "die! die!"
and finally
it did
and I felt ashamed
of myself
because I knew
then
how badly that chipmunk,
like me,
had wanted to live.

Christmas Morn

I woke and poked
my little brother
and he followed me
down to the living room
piled neck-high with presents
like the cave of Ali Baba
and then Gramp's voice
boomed "get back in those beds!"
and we crept back up
like condemned prisoners
to await a pardon
from Grandma who
gave us the okay
but said not to open gifts
until Uncle Al got up,
but he never did;
"must have celebrated too much"
Grandma said;
we dug in,
tore the paper
to shreds:
I got the black figure skates
I'd asked for
plus a book of Shakespeare's plays
from my sister
which I never read
because
I did not know Shakespeare
from Shitmore.

2

ocean waves of
stuporous languor —
the maid sweeps the sun deck

Moving Man

I worked a day laborer job
as moving man
and carried box after box
of books
out of a professor's house
and into a truck
parked on a tree-lined street
in Ann Arbor, Michigan;
the guy working with me
took it easy
and carried out about half of what
I did
and at one point I told the guy to
get a move-on
and he looked at me like I was
crazy
and maybe I was
and late in the afternoon
the truck driver gave me some shit
for slowing down
and I went off on him,
a screaming fit,
and he blanched
and said that he knew
what my problem was
and he handed me an extra ten
but
lack of money was not
my real problem —
the world was.

The Stripper

I worked security
and sat at a desk
in the lobby
of a hotel
in Kenmore Square,
Boston,
and had people
sign in & out.
A black girl who
worked in the Combat Zone
and who looked like Hayley Mills
the actress
came in early A.M.
and would lean over
the desk to sign in
and I would look down
her dress
and she thought it funny
but I did not
and one morning she
asked me to let her into
her room because
she had lost her key
and we rode up in an elevator
lit by her broad smile
and I opened her door
and said "there you go"
and she gave me an angry
look as she went inside
and I was troubled afterward
until I realized what the look
meant and what I had missed
but there was no going back

and I had to endure
her bitter redress
in the mornings,
but I never did
stop looking.

The Maid

After my grandmother
went into the hospital
my grandfather hired a maid,
Lena,
big as a refrigerator
her silver hair parted in the
middle of her skull and
plastered to her head
like a shower cap;
she took the nearly empty
catsup bottle and
ran water from the faucet
into it
and returned it to the table;
after dinner she encouraged
the four of us kids
to beat each other with the pillows
we were not allowed to touch,
and she roared with laughter
as we slipped and slid
across the linoleum,
it was the only time
the four of us ever did
something fun together
but the fun ended
when my grandfather walked in
his face grave as sin
and hawk nose pointed at Lena
who laughed at him
too.

3

a drunken Indian on the bus
says to me
"football player!"

Wife-Beater

The jail cell was thin and
long;
I sat at one end
and a wife-beater
at the other.
The wife-beater paced the floor
back and forth;
he was tall and thin and had crazy eyes;
whenever he came near
I stared him down.
I wondered if I would
have to beat on him:
Maybe that was why
they put me in there.
I did not care who he had beat;
I had no opinion on his case;
hell,
I wasn't even married.

Paddy Wagon

Running down a dark
rain-slick street
chased by
two big guys from the bar,
my shoe fell off
onto the cobblestones
and I stopped
to pick it up,
because I owned only one pair,
and one of the guys
grabbed me
and pinned my arms
and the other wailed
punches,
George Foreman style,
the bite of the guy's ring on
my scalp,
his fist's flashing
past my face
like other lives
the beating went on
and on
until the paddy wagon arrived
and the guys and a cop
threw me inside
onto a mat
like the ones they used to use
in gym class
in Junior High
and I lay back
as the wagon rattled
and streetlights flashed through
a screen window

and I remembered how much
I disliked Junior High,
except for gym class.

Flusterated

I spent all my money
in a bar
trying to pick-up a chick
who would not look me
in the eye
and I walked out of the joint
into the cold dark street
at 2 A.M.
broke
with nowhere to go
except home to my bed
of sorrows;
and then two girls walked out of the shadows
one on either side of a guy
and I said "hey, you" to one of the girls
and she said "bug off!"
and something snapped inside me
I don't know what
and I grabbed the guy
by his hair—
he was a hippy bastard--
and I flung him down
and the girls screamed
and the guy got up
and charged me
but with his head down
like a dope
and I caught him with an uppercut
and he dropped
at my feet
and then the blue lights of a cop car
lit-up the trees and the night
and I started to think-up

a story
to tell to my probation officer
because I knew that
I was back in the shit.

Maybe

I should have stayed
in the bar
drinking beer
until I fell off the stool
and died
on the floor
like Baldy Sherman
did
or else died out back
in a Room For Rent
like Buzzy
my Uncle's buddy
an ex-Green Beret
who left
nothing
but his carcass;
he came to the house one
Christmas day
and he and my Uncle
spent all afternoon
drinking beer
and smoking cigarettes
in the sun parlor
while trying to put together an electric train
set
that
like them
never got on track.

The Fix

It's a nowhere trip
to the starting gate—
your horse has already bolted
so you start
to run
the track
and the fucker is endless
and every so often
the horses come around
and run over you
and you get back up
(have to)
and shoot for place or show
because winning has been long forgot
but most of the time the best
you can do
is to keep going,
that's it…
and the race
hell,
it's fixed anyway.

4

another email from
Olive Garden —
what does she want now?

zen he went to the market
zen he came home

Molder

A squirrel in the park,
plump,
7 to 8 inches in height,
svelte gray coat,
attacked and bit a girl
who later died
and the cops went berserk
guns blasting
and killed two hundred squirrels
but none of the witnesses
to the attack
could positively ID the perp
so the cops put out an APB with
an artist's sketch of
the killer squirrel
which brought 1000 calls
into the station
but
as of this writing
the suspect remains at large
possibly
up a tree
or
in some hole in a wall.

Mush

Trudging downhill as
a cold wind cuts
through
my four layers of clothing
I meet the Abdomiable Snowman
on the corner and say "how-do?"
and he says
"John? No, you're not John"
and I say
"no shit, Shakespeare
I'm Sergeant Preston
of the Royal Canadian Mounties"
and I move on
with a "mush" to my huskies,
but
hey
this ain't Nome, Alaska
man,
though
it could be, I guess
the way the cold breath
and scarfs wrapped around heads
and over-exposure at ten below
could mean death
with snow from Yukon drifts
and squalls
in Wite-Outville.

Savior

With the money from my
McArthur grant
I bought a truck load of AK-47's
and loaded them onto
a rented Boeing 747 and
crash-landed the plane
in the Gaza strip and
started handing the weapons
out the back door
and all the people there
praised my name
and loved me like a savior
except for the Hamas bastards
who did not want me around
to louse-up their martyrdom racket
so kicked my ass
into Egypt
where the Muslim Brotherhood
did not think much of me
either.

Poison Gas

I wrote a letter
to Basher Assad in Syria
asking for
some poison gas
because
I want to use some
on the neighbors
they're all sons a bitches around here
even the parolees across the street,
gas them too
and do the town as well —
a bunch of bastards —
and while I'm at it
hell
might as well do myself.

Left Jab

He was a Sam Langford type guy
only 5′ 7″ but
could really punch,
fists felt like hammer blows
"the toughest little son-of-a-bitch
who ever lived" Jack Johnson said.
Grew out instead
of up—
he had to get inside though
or perish
at the end of a tall man's fists
like the jab of that Russian guy
what's his name—
Putin
whose reach extends to
the Ukraine
and above and beyond.

Any More Questions?

"How do you get to the cemetery?"
the guy with a camera and tie
asks.
"Well," I say
"you got to die first,
then they carry you there
in a box
and plant you
somewhere,
according to whatever
your name,
then they put a rock
over the top of you
and charge you
for the rock
and the plot
and the box,
and then they give you a hair-cut
every once in awhile
plus a drink,
and there you remain
for perpetuity,
which
is a long goddamn time."

9 Billion Years

The sun only has another
9 billion years
to burn:
what do we do when it
starts to turn red?
get the fuck out
of here,
fly to Mars maybe
until it too burns,
and then?
Have to tow the moon with us
and launch that sucker
outward
until the sun
cools its jets
and somebody
can come up
with some
heat and light.

Nehru jackets

Rainy day in South Florida,
the beaches empty
sidewalks puddled
palm trees flailing
against fate;
I sit in a hotel room
and listen to oldies on the radio,
70's pop tunes, disco fever
stuff
and remember
my bell bottom slacks
and platform shoes
and hair to my shoulders
and how cool I looked
even if
I never
was.

Bait

Sun setting on Key West, Florida
where Hemingway lived
my old buddy
until the day on his boat
he said we were going spear fishing
and I said "no way — I'm not going"
and he said "get your gear on, kid"
and I said "don't get tough with me, Hem
or I'll drop you like a bad habit,"
and he thought that funny
and told me stay on the boat
if I wanted
but not drink all the gin
save some for him
but once I got started on
the stuff I could not stop
and when Hem got back
he was pissed and him
and Manuel, who once fought Sugar Ray
in the Garden, tied me up
and trolled me as bait
behind the boat
across the estuary
trying to catch a shark
and I sobered
quick
and shouted "Hem you prick!"
and he laughed
and cut me loose
and I crawled to shore

using my toes as flippers
like the first fish
to become amphibian.

5

I told her I'd been seeing
a blonde
with big tits
and she said
"is that what matters to you,
the size of the breasts?"
and I said "yes"
and she laughed
as I gazed
at her chest.

"its been that kind of day,"
the woman said
after returning to the store
for her pocketbook

The Girl and the Greek

She was a good girl but
headstrong,
had to have her own way
and one day her boss
in the restaurant
underpaid her by ten bucks
and she went and opened the
cash register
and took out a ten
and the boss
a Greek with a bushy moustache
grabbed her
and I grabbed him
slammed him against a wall
tore the buttons off his shirt
and asked,
as I held him by the throat,
did he want to fuck with someone?
and he said "no"
very humbly and
un-boss like
and I let him go
and then
the girl and me
we went back to our place
and fucked.

Ma Cherie Amore

Shut-up Mr. Radioman
and play some Stevie Wonder
like they used to do
in '67
over the loudspeaker
at Anthony's Pool
where I stood in the ice-cold
shallows with my girl
whose hand I held
as we crept into the water
she wearing a bikini
and with breasts the size
of tangerines
that I could not touch
because she said no,
No, and NO,
she was a good Catholic girl
I was a bastard;
she bawled
when I told her
that
it was over.

Date

I went out with a black girl,
a sharp chick
and funny
who all my friends wanted to
fuck
but none had the guts to be seen
out on a date with her;
I borrowed my brother's car
and took her to the outdoor movies
and we made-out
in the back seat;
her mouth was bigger than
mine—
like a cave
my tongue and lips
got lost in.

Odd

She was nice but
a little odd;
did not shave her
arm pits or legs
or wash her underwear,
and one night
after we had been together a week
we drank some scotch
and went to bed
and I had a nightmare
of flying saucers
invading
and knew
in the morning
that I had to end it
and told her
and she cried
a little
and said "I still think you're a neat guy,"
and that was
the end
of it.

Boston Cream

Sometimes I go to Dunkin' Donuts
for coffee
and while in line
think about the doughnuts
maybe even consider a crueler
or plain stick
sometimes fantasize about
a Boston Cream
which
I would never order
because of my diabetes
or a chocolate glazed
either
it's the same as
thinking about Miss America
in my bed
with her legs spread
a far-out fantasy
that cannot be sustained
but
what about a reduced fat muffin,
it is a possibility,
one less remote
than
the beauty queen.

6

spasmodic second hand of the clock
on the wall of the doctor's
waiting room

Water

Cold Army-green river
that Fred slipped into
below the barely opaque
surface that wrote his
death certificate in frothy
curlicues like Arabic
though he was Polish I
think, but don't know.
He always said hello like
we were best friends
though I did not even
know his last name;
he swam out of the picture
frame and came-up fish-gray
on the shore. He wore a suit
jacket and looked Asiatic.
He smoked Camels or Lucky
Strikes non-filter. Had brown
nicotine stains on his fingers.
He spoke so slowly you had
to finish his sentences for him.

Spring Training

I did not like playing baseball
in the Spring
because it was cold
in New England in April
and catching the ball in
the palm of the glove
stung my hand like the bite of a spider
and hitting the ball anywhere but
on the meat of the bat
felt as if I'd splintered my fingers
it was in the heat
when I felt best
when the sweat oiled my
limbs
unhinged arms
and I grew wings
to sail
with the white ball
over distant fences
to dreamed-of lands.

Rights

In Cambridge, Massachusetts, outside
The Mug & Muffin Restaurant
a guy wearing a pork pie hat was
singing "Sixteen Tons"
for spare change
as another guy
over by the newspaper kiosk
poured gasoline from a can
over his head then asked passersby for a match
and some jackass gave him one
and some waitress screamed
and the guy with gasoline was
tackled
and as I moved ahead
against a tide of liberals
fleeing
as if for life
a girl with terror-dazed eyes
ran into my chest,
and the guy,
pinned to the ground,
screamed
"I want my rights!"
as if
setting himself on fire
in public
was one.

Okra

Working too much
lately;
going to have a heart
attack ack ack
and be back in the
dreary hospital
and asked to rate my
pain, one to ten
"sixteen"
and watching from
the window
the dull ache of day
while some guy
in the next bed
watches "Oprah."

Frozen

We had stopped at Hardee's Burgers
on our way back to the college
and some high school hot-shot
wearing a football jacket
in the parking lot
punched Phil in the face
and Phil grabbed the guy
by the guy's collar
and shouted
"cut it out!"
but the guy kept punching
his fists
splat
whap
splat
and Phil shouted louder
"CUT IT OUT!"
and blood began to stream
down Phil's face
and I said "hit him!
Hit him Phil!"
but Phil only screamed
"Jesus Christ, stop it!"
and the guy's fists
whap
whap
splat
finally stopped
and Phil let go
and back in the car
where Steve and Ron
had sat
during the fight

Phil was asked
"why didn't you hit him?"
and Phil, a bloody mess
and blowing bubbles out of his nose,
said
"I don't know."

Zero

I woke cold
beneath a
wool blanket
and had bad thoughts
about the landlord
the dirty old
and hurried to
put on clothes
then
sat at the computer
to check emails
but
none to check
and I wondered why
no response
to the poems
I sent
out into the snow
and ice
and ten below east coast weather —
did they all
get
the cold shoulder?

Rat Race

Driving a rental car up Route 1
along the Florida coast
cars darting in and out
across three lanes
a sign up ahead
tells me to get into the left lane
but when I start to turn
a car behind
boxes me in at the light,
a pale-faced glasses-wearing prick
who looks straight ahead
"hey ASSHOLE!" I shout, "thanks a lot, ASSHOLE!"
a woman driver of sagacity
behind me smiles,
probably thinks I am a road-rage nut
but I am just a little uptight
and when the light changes
I squeeze into the left lane
in front of a car
that almost rams me
and make my turn
and escape
until the next intersection.

The Sub-Mariner (Marvell Comics Super-hero)

The Sub-Mariner, sixty-plus years old
is sinking;
he's still got the little wings
and the Max Baer body
but he's not as quick
as he used to be
and he's gulping for air
some days
though still powerful
but routinely late
now
to the scene,
like cops
who stop for doughnuts
he gets there
in his own sweet time,
moving like a manta ray
with arms outstretched
as if crucified…
The seas grew too big
too violent
like capitalism
and he began to know
fear —
the shark, the barracuda, the electric eel
he used to drive away
like they were children
no longer move at
his approach
and even the walrus,
whose whiskers
he's adopted
plus the wrinkled skin

does not move for him —
everything has changed
and the Sub-Mariner
does not know
if it's for the better.

Snoop

A cop followed me into the driveway
blue lights flashing
"do you know why I stopped you?"
"no idea"
"because your muffler is loud"
"because your mother eats shit" I told myself
as his flashlight played
over me
like the glance of an ice queen—
"any outstanding warrants on your license?"
"no"
I had my shit together
(unlike the last time I was stopped)
he gave me my license
back without even
checking it out.
The blue lights faded.
What did the fucker want?
A donation to the Police Benevolent Society?

Pop

I punched my brother
in the face
as we stood toe to toe
in the backyard;
Mr. Larson came out of
his house next door
and said "cut that out!"
He stood between us
pot-bellied and
with skin like a cured ham;
my brother and I
drifted apart
and Mr. Larson went back
to his shit-colored house
to his wife he did not allow
outdoors
to his kids who called him "Pop"
to his carport where
he sat in summer drinking the beer
he made in his cellar
to his lawn he mowed three times a week;
he had a nasal twang to his voice
like the voice of someone
from
somewhere else.

NORTH

Drying October leaves like
clenched fists
holding onto the trees…
I am coming to the end of
Céline's NORTH
his tragic-clown-chronicle
of his post-collabo days when
he, his wife Lilli, his friend
and fellow fascist Le Vig,
and Bébert the cat, also
fascist, fled France and lived
as "Franzosen" in Prussia,
protected by remaining Nazis,
ones not dying in Berlin, 1944.
Quite a trip…the good doctor
Destouches…the racist Céline…
his apocalyptic style of three
dots…three Franzosen…they've
kept me company…800 pages…
me, alone in Vermont…I'm not
complaining…not at all…just a
fact…like the leaves…dying,
clinging to the trees
with my fingertips.

7

walking along the beach
my sore feet—
the moon wrapped in gauze

dry leaves slither on their bellies
along the pavement—
my father in the war

The Pier

I walked out to the end of the pier
to visit with the birds
who inched-over for me
and we all stood
placidly
facing the sun
and the birds cooed
until some guy
strode
determinedly
and I inched-over for him
and the birds scattered
as if from a big wind
and the guy looked over
the edge of the pier
at the pale green water
same as everywhere,
and then he turned and left
and the birds returned
one by one
and we all stood
facing the sun
and the birds
started
to coo
again.

Diner

I like places that
have a counter
where a single guy
like me
can sit
and a gum-chewing wise-cracking
waitress
to shoot the shit
and a newspaper
nearby
and something to eat
that won't upset
and maybe a jukebox —
though that's a stretch —
and customers who
appreciate my wit
and who know when to keep
their mouths shut
and when to open.

208$

My lottery number came in,
paid 208$;
the machine at the liquor store
lit-up, whistled, and
said "winner! winner!"
and a guy in line,
who had a lean and
hungry look,
said "congratulations."
The clerk counted-out the
bills one by one
into my palm
and I put the winnings
into my pocket
and left out the side door
in case the guy
was waiting out front.

Burke's Inn

Out of the loop,
2 A.M.
eyes propped open
with toothpicks
and reading
in bed
the bed starts to float
then sink
and I am back at my Grandfather's bar
BURKE'S INN
a big new neon sign out front
and now a mall attached to the back
plus extra storeys on top
and plush carpets,
chandeliers,
and I see my Aunt
who does not recognize me
(she never did)
and she says "a thousand dollars…
a thousand dollars…" like an idiot,
and then I am upstairs
where a pregnant woman
lies on a table
naked beneath a sheet
I take a peek
underneath;
I do not know who she is
or even
who I am.

12:41 A.M.

I sit in the kitchen and
listen to Mozart
on the radio, the music
like a fluttering butterfly going
nowhere purposefully.
I wear only underwear and
have my feet up on the table
where my computer sits, screen
black as licorice. I think I will hit
the sack, but before beddy-bye
write on a pad of paper yellow
as a sick canary. The walls of
this place are anemic white—
as if past tenants tried to suck
out the life: now I am trying to
put some back. My stack of
poems: that is life. My drawings
taped to the walls: more of the
same. My books on the shelf:
ditto. The rest, including me,
is some kind of illusion.

Advice

Almost fell on my face
on the way to the
bathroom
at 5 A.M.
to answer the call
of nature
that I could not ignore
like I can the telephone
DRING
dring
while
I am taking a nap
while
I am on the toilet
while
I am having immortal thoughts:
hello?...hello?
it is President Obama calling
to ask me for advice
says he will send a limousine
over
so I wait
and wake
to rain
on the windows
and everywhere else.

Reality

Sat on a bench in the sunshine
and the whole human race
went by me
in trucks and cars and
on foot and
I did not give a
fuck about any of it
except the sun
on my face,
my jacket pulled tightly
in place:
November, winter on the
way;
I got up and walked and
met my friend
Marcus (Aurelius) and
I said "it's cold' and
he said "it will be cold from now
until June" and I said
"thanks a lot" and
he said "it is reality"
and I walked on
not wanting to deal
with reality
so early in the day.

Voice

The only thing that could ruin
this moment
is a human's voice
and here it comes
wearing a camouflage coat
and red-eyed
swollen
speaking Spanish
beneath a baseball cap
without designation
like him
from barrios in other time zones
his mouth
to the maw
of the telephone
he snaps shut
on "adios"
and once again
perfect silence
reigns
as the music
plays
overhead.

Stopped

Had a headlight out
and got stopped
by a cop
who politely and unnecessarily
introduced himself as
he shined his light
on my expired sticker
then asked for my license
which I gave him,
but not my insurance card
which I could not find,
and he went away
then returned
and said my license had expired too
and he asked me to step out of the car
into the street
where I stood
exposed in the glare of headlights
and I wondered
what else
I had not been
paying attention to.

Fragile

I brush my teeth
with boric acid,
shave my ass
and walk backwards;
watch lunatics pick
through garbage;
everyone I know
is serious as Ebola;
I'm stuck on the road
less traveled;
I send my letters
marked FRAGILE.
When alone I bottle
dew and play
with my marbles.

Twilight

and the city hushed;
a somber hue
of shadowed-ness.
Scars of the brick buildings
hidden,
wrinkles folded-in for night.
Black birds on the wing
beneath a charcoal sky
with pink ribbon.

2 Oh One

my weight
that's good
though
I still have
the hunger
to eat
all sorts of
delicious crap
that plugs my
arteries
and will,
no doubt,
shorten my
existence
here
on
Planet
Crouton.

Jackass

Trouble at the door of
Dunkin' Donuts:
a guy smiling like a
happy jackass
stands holding the door open
for me
and
when I fail to say
"thank you"
or anything else
his happy face turns to
mud
like the coffee served inside
and he snidely says
"you're welcome!"
to which
I reply
"get bent!"
and all his happiness
disappears into
the uncouth bowl
of jackass
life.

8

six poems accepted in a week:
I walk like a Chief
through this squaw town

sir sir sir
that's all
I hear
here

1:30 P.M.

Mist and gray splotches of
clouds
swimming into the
dreary wonder of
a December afternoon
and settling down
among crenellated ridge lines
of black skeletal trees
like Transylvanian Vladimir
castles
fading in
fading out —
the misty ghosts of
Christmases.

Same Oh

Got a break:
a week away
from this place,
and now I am back
and see
that
the old dump
has not changed:
same characters and places to avoid,
same attitudes of indifference,
same lack of anything approaching liveliness,
same incrustation,
same cracks in the facades;
the train whistle sounds the same
so do the sirens;
the same amount of staring going on
as before;
same everything,
nothing has changed:
nothing can.

Cheap Living

I live cheap in this 3 room
apartment
on the second floor of nowhere
among books and pictures
and my poems
and the telephone directory
and bottles of pills
on a table
cluttered as a city block
and the landlord absent on Mars
an hour away by car
though his brother
a decent sort,
unlike the shifty son-of-a-gun
landlord,
lives next door
in case of a problem
which I have
on occasion
like the day the toilet chain broke
like the night water from the roof ran down a wall
but usually
I got no problems
at all
except for what goes on
in between
my ears.

Punk Fight

The screaming starts
and grows in volume
as two punks get ready
to duke it out;
one punk wings
round-house rights
the other dances
with fists upheld
like John L. Sullivan.
The fights goes on and on
like a bad play;
a girl is called "crack whore"
a guy "bitch"
and John L. Sullivan
spits on his opponent.
The cops are eating doughnuts
or else playing cards
in the station;
the crowd grows to two dozen,
all hoping for a better show
or a quicker end
and when a moon-faced cop shows
the punks split
and when the cop
sweating through his shirt
asks
what I'd seen
I say "nothing"
but he gets an earful from
the fat girl
working at the hot dog stand.

Townie

Hanging around this dirty old
town
thinking of starting a fight
with someone
so I can knock
them down;
maybe beat-up an
old man drunk
or choke a gray-haired
church cunt,
or bomb City Hall
or walk up onto the overpass
and drop cobble stones,
or set the library on fire
or rip somebody's head off
or
maybe just think of
what I might do,
if things get bad enough —
if they don't stop blowing
that goddamn train whistle.

Backyard

I want
a private spot
to sit
and read
or write
or
take a nap,
feed the birds,
keep a cat,
play in the dirt
if I want to;
study the shadows
the sunlight makes;
a little table
to put my coffee cup on,
a view of sky
and quiet time,
all I like
all I can get,
that's it.

Slog

Dried skin on
my scalp;
I rub creams on
but none help—
48 hours of sunshine would cure
me
but there is no sun,
no moon either,
no stars,
and little love;
a gray plenitude of
fog,
impenetrable sky of
sludge
dull as years spent in
cribs of
babyhood;
dirty as the dish rag
grandma used to wipe
the sink with;
northeast-gray the pigeons
fly through;
swilled soup-of-the-day
with glops of charcoal
and lead; I rub some on
my head and
it feels good
in a kind of strange,
and maybe sick,
way.

9

no check in the mail:
mailbox empty as
the Grand Canyon

the suckerfish
pushes up daisies
in the garden

leaves jump up and run
like little fools
out into the busy highway

Wing Tips

new wing tip shoes
on the table,
notebook on my lap,
symphony number
whatever by Franz
Haydn on the radio,
crescendo to climax;
my polyester pants
are black like my shoes
wrist watch hi ho
silver.

Descent to New York

of flight number
whatever
sinking fast
like a bad dinner
a woman beside me
reads a KINDLE
I try and read her
but can't
the plane is tilting
floundering in a sea of
bounding stewardesses
up and down the aisle;
sun-bathed blue sky outside the
window
like a glimpse of Heaven;
my ears compress and
pop;
the unwieldy contraption
wallows down
and lands
THUMP
"a rough landing" I say
to the pilot
as I leave
"no" he says
"a La Guardia landing."

Notebook

The notebook slips from
my hands
and runs across the table
and I chase it down
and chain it to my palm
but it breaks the lock
and lands in my lap
and I pick it up
and bite it
and the taste
is bitter,
but I like it.

Art

No kids
no wife;
sometimes it seems
as if life
is not worth
the living,
and like I missed the boat
somewhere
but then
whenever I start to write
I think
that this art is what
I have to love:
as fickle as it is
as un-glamorous in the
morning
as moody in the night
as meaningless as it
sometimes seems —
in all its flaws
and wrinkles
it still comes through
for me,
still there
whenever I reach
for it,
from the dark
or from the most desolate
shore.

Hi-Ho

I'm the Lone Ranger
after Tonto died
after Silver ran off
after the mills shut down
and the welfare state came around
and chain stores and malls
moved in
and Mom and Pops' moved out
and nobody knew their neighbors
anymore
and heroin became the new
pot
and men started to wear earrings
and women got tattoos on their chests
and the good jobs went overseas
and cities went under
and heroes
like me
could no longer find
work
because nobody trusted a masked-man
anymore.

Meck-A-Nick

Stood and watched the mechanic
beads of sweat on his neck
curses under his breath;
screw gun shit the bed
on him
lug nut stripped;
used tires stacked against
the garage wall
threads worn smooth
as a baby's bottom;
I thought of my father
Ed
Manager of a Flying A
Mobil Gasoline station,
and of the white horse
Pegasus
rearing on back legs
outside of the office door.

Exist

Sitting in my shorts
in the kitchen of
my apartment
a fan blowing on my flesh
brown from
golden sun;
writing these words for
whomever might read them
maybe only me
what difference if
these words go elsewhere
or not,
I've no one I want to impress,
do not have to produce,
no tenure riding on these
lines,
nothing
but my self-respect
and to bear witness
I guess
that I lived
that I was alive.

10

I am alone with my art
until the stars come out
then I'll have company
of sparkling minions
in the hundred-millions.

light beam from the
kitchen bulb,
the sword of Excalibur:
I pick it up and
slice my way
to a pearly gate
that opens
with
a sesame

Lumbago?

I lived in a basement room in Drumcondra, a working class suburb of Dublin. Drumcondra looked forbiddingly ugly; no grass, no trees, and dark: burnt brown houses of the same shape lined shoulder-to-shoulder with angled peaked roofs, the roofs looking like a crenellated fortress wall.

My room was cold. I fed 25-pence pieces into a wall meter for heat. Never enough heat; never enough 25-pence pieces...A baby in the apartment above cried almost continuously—cried as if being tortured. One day I'd had enough of the crying and went upstairs and knocked on the apartment door. I was pissed. The door opened. A guy wearing a white t-shirt and baggy pants stood in the doorway. He looked like a remnant of Neanderthal man: prognathous jaw, heavily ridged brow, concave eye sockets...I was afraid. I became meek; my voice mild. He smirked at me. My complaint turned into apology. He shut the door in my face.

I spent little time in my room. A lot of time in the pubs. Drinking Guinness stout and Irish whiskey in the pubs. I was shit-faced every night. One night I fell on the floor of the Dublin-Drumcondra bus and could not get up. Lead weights held me down. Other passengers lifted me upright; they were smiling—I was putting on a show for them. I tried to tell the people how much I loved them but the words did not come out right. I was a happy drunk. I loved everybody. I walked around laughing my ass off. One night a guy in the Kentucky Fried Chicken joint on the corner of my street—I'd stopped to buy fries with gravy—asked if I was high. "No," I said, "I'm drunk."

After waking one morning, I looked into the mirror and did a double-take. My face did not look right. I took a closer look: My eyes were yellow as egg yolks. What the fuck? Did I have the flu? I wondered. Did I have...malaria?

Construction

Jimmy held the fucking board in place and screwed a fucking screw into the fucking board. The fucker held. Good. He looked at his watch. Fifteen fucking minutes to lunchtime. He set his fucking screw gun on the fucking floor. Took his fucking level out of his fucking belt and checked the fucking board. Fucking level. About fucking time he got something fucking right, he told himself. He stepped back, looked at the fucking window case. Good fucking job, even if he did say so himself...

Ten more fucking minutes to lunch. Too fucking late, he thought, to start another fucking window case. He glanced over his shoulder. Looking for Fred, the fucking prick. Nowhere in fucking sight. Good. He'd fuck off for ten minutes, he thought, then go to lunch.

He sat in the Port-o-let and smoked a butt. Had to quit the fucking butts, he told himself. Two fucking packs a day: no fucking wonder he couldn't fucking breath. Fucking butt smelled better than fucking Port-o-let though. Fucking Port-o-let smelled like Clorox and shit...He read the graffiti on the fucking Port-o-let wall. Most of it about Fred the fucking prick. Some about fucking Fred the prick's mother. Fred had come out of her asshole, Jimmy thought, not her cunt--why he, Fred, was such a shithead. Ha ha! Should write that down, Jimmy thought. Fuck it: he was too fucking tired to make the effort. He shot his butt into the crapper. It was lunchtime. Fuckin' A!

Creatures Come Out At Night

After hiking all day I reached the shelter at dusk and unrolled my sleeping bag on the lean-to floor and lay down and went to sleep. Sometime later I woke to the sound of some creature gnawing on the shelter, seemingly eating its way through the floor below me. What was it? Rabbit? Beaver? I went back to sleep and woke, this time to the sound of dogs barking. I turned my flashlight on and saw the silhouette of a bulky shaped thing with spikes sitting at the foot of my sleeping bag. The thing's quilled matted back made a sort of design of concentric circles, something like a bulls-eye. I screamed and slashed my walking stick down on the shelter floor. The porcupine turned its head toward me then slowly strolled, its quills rattling, along the edge of the floor, and dropped down. I played my light out into the clearing before the shelter. Porcupines as far as I could see, standing on hind legs, frolicking or motionless; the bark of the creatures sounding like a dog's bark; and up on the lip of the shelter above, where I shone my light, more porcupines, their heads hung over the shelter's lip, eyes glittering; plus still more clinging, like gargoyles, to the shelter's sides, all heads turned my way...I would stay awake until dawn, I told myself. I would not chance becoming a human pin cushion. What would I do if, for some reason, the things came after me? Some of those out front looked to be big as hogs and cows. Would my stick be sufficient to keep them off? I turned my light off to save batteries, and...I woke. The porkies had moved back onto the shelter floor, a line of them on the floor edge like cats on a fence post. I screamed and slashed my stick: They ignored me. I stood and waved the stick above their heads. If I struck one, would it retaliate? Would other porkies swarm en masse in defense of the assaulted one? I lay back down. My flashlight, I noted, was becoming dim. Soon it would be useless. Some of the creatures on the edge, I noted, seemed to be taking an inordinate interest in me, nodding their little snouts in my direction. Or was I imagining such things? My mind playing tricks? I became groggy; my eyes began to close...I woke, shuddering. The porkies lay or sat singly or in groups all around me, their bristling quills close enough for me to touch. A fat one scrambled aside as I sat up. In the distance, over the heads of the congregation, I saw a streak of gray in the dark sky. I felt as if rescue were at hand. Soon, the pitch dark night would end!!

Big Spender

My Uncle Al, the Big Spender (on himself: flashy silk clothes, big car—he's lived at home all his life, thirty years) has decided, since he's forgotten our birthdays, to take the bunch of us out and blow us to a feed at Florence's Diner in Northampton. Grandma, Sister, my brother Butch, me, and Uncle Al—he drives us down to the diner (known for its fresh seafood) in his car, a tan and silver Buick Electra (push button windows, vinyl seat covers, V-8 tape player). As usual, the place is packed; we sit in a horseshoe shaped booth of red Naugahyde. My Uncle wears a fancy suit-coat and tie and he's smiling, something he rarely does at home. A waitress comes to our table with menus. Uncle Al nods at me and says loudly: "See, I told you they had a lot of pretty girls in Northampton." I don't remember him talking to me about girls. The waitress, a red-head in a starched white uniform, does not seem displeased by the remark. Uncle Al, for some reason, does not look as fat or as lonely to me as he usually does. "Sit up!" Grandma scolds Sister, "and get your hair out of your eyes!" Sister tugs at her bangs, shoots Grandma a dirty look. The waitress awaits our order. Butch says he'll have a hot dog; Grandma decides to splurge, go all out: she orders a hot roast beef sandwich; sister says she does not want anything—she's on a diet and plus, it's obvious, she can't stand the thought of eating in pubic with us. Grandma begs Sister not to make a spectacle of herself and to order something, "For Pete's Sake!" and "The Love of God!" Who is Pete, I wonder. "Cheeseburger and fries," Sister says like she is ordering poison. Uncle Al, who has told us we could order anything (I did hear him say that) says he will have a steak, medium rare (like the Big Spenders eat them). "And you?" the waitress says, meaning me. "I'll have the swordfish." Uncle Al's smile fades faster than a rock thrown into a pond; he stares at me across the horseshoe. "Go'wan," Grandma says caustically, "you don't want swordfish!" She smiles—the top shelf of her pearl-white dentures remind me of piano keys. "Yes, I do." Uncle Al stares. The waitress taps her pencil on her order pad. "You better eat all of it," Uncle Al says, pissed-off.

The fish arrives—an inch thick, big as a platter; juice runs off of it in streams—Grandma asks for a piece, just a taste. Why didn't she order her own fish? I don't ask. Uncle Al is still staring: I've cost him twelve bucks and he's never going to forget it.

Acknowledgements:

The author would like to gratefully acknowledge the following publications, where some of the pieces in this book first appeared: The Commonline Journal, Meat For Tea, Lipstick Party Magazine, Toasted Cheese, Boston Poetry magazine, Dead Snakes, VerseWrights, HAPPY, Fuck Fiction, Kind of a Hurricane Press Anthology (The Four Seasons, Objects in the Rear View Mirror), Slim Body Anthology (This Body I Live In), High Coupe, Ink Sweat & Tears, the WORLD, Rain, L'amour Fou, 63 Channels, The Periphery, and The Literary Commune.

About the Author:

Wayne F. Burke was born in Adams, Massachusetts and raised by his paternal grandparents. As a boy he was an All-Star baseball player, and in High School an All Class-A football player. He attended the University of Massachusetts—where he was a member of the freshman football team—and three other institutions of higher learning before graduating from Goddard College in 1979. His work history includes stints as bartender, moving man, cook, machine shop operator, sign painter, substitute school teacher, carpenter, truck driver, book reviewer (for the Burlington Free Press newspaper, Burlington, Vermont), and, for the past four years, LPN in a nursing home. His stories, essays, reviews, and poems have appeared in numerous publications. He has two other collections of poetry, published by BareBackPress: *Words that Burn* (2013), and *Dickhead* (2015).

Also by Wayne F. Burke

Words That Burn
$12.00
132 pages
6 x 9
ISBN-13: 978-0992035518
ISBN-10: 0992035511
BISAC: Poetry / General
BareBackPress

Praise for Words That Burn

"One of the most unapologetically honest books I have read...A poet who takes no prisoners, pulls no punches, wastes no words and knows how to tell a good story...Burke not only has the guts to admit his part in the fractured society he makes comment on, he also has the audacity to make art out of it...A sane voice in a mad world."
~ Matthew J. Hall,
Screaming With Brevity

"...the brutal evisceration of one man's experience of life on the planet earth. Burke writes with confidence, and swag...unforgettable imagery, black humor...something in these experiences that everyone can, or will, relate to."
~ Peter Jelen, author of
Impressions Of An Expatriate

"Burke is a tough young poet who, like all the rest of us, has learned some lessons from William Carlos Williams, but without imitating Williams. Burke writes the language of where he came from and with respect for it, and more power to him."
~ Alan Dugan,
Winner of *The National Book Award*
and the *Prix de Rome*.

Dickhead
$13.00
108 pages
5.25 x 8
ISBN-13: 978-1926449050
ISBN-10: 1926449053
BISAC: Poetry / General
BareBackPress

Praise for Dickhead

"These are wonderful, honest, hard-hitting poems. I loved every single one. NO ONE ELSE is writing poems like this, rooted in the real world, and with such a powerful voice."
~ Howard Frank Mosher,
*author of A Stranger in the Kingdom
and Walking to Gatlinburg*

"DICKHEAD is full of paradoxical twists, wordplay, subtle associations and darkly funny atmosphere. (Burke) is an earthy pragmatist with a surreal inner life...an insomniac dreamer."
~ Ada Fetters, Editor,
The Commonline Journal

"...a monster among us, a dangerous beast...reads like the best of Bukowski. Dead serious, no nonsense and it feels absolutely true. Burke swaggers through with such confidence you could almost resent his elan."
~ Michael Dennis,
Today's Book of Poetry

"DICKHEAD is about becoming a man, it's about the boy inside who still skips and sings, it's about the grind and coming to terms with self, it's about fantasy, reality, connection, ugliness and beauty; most importantly though, it is a book and a body of work that asks more questions than it answers. The word genius is bandied about far too freely, and most geniuses are not recognized as such in their life time. With that being said I am not the least bit hesitant in claiming Burke's poetic genius and I hope it is recognized in his lifetime."
~ Matthew J. Hall,
Screaming With Brevity

www.barebackpress.com

www.ingramcontent.com/pod-product-compliance
Lightning Source LLC
Chambersburg PA
CBHW060333050426
42449CB00011B/2744